Chakra Magic

Christine Keleny

CKBooks

No parts of this book may be reproduced or used in any form without permission except for brief quotations used for articles, posts or in reviews.

Contact Christine Keleny and see all of her books at christinekelenybooks.com.
Contact the illustrator, Marianella Aguirre, at kiwimary.com

LCCN 2018953600
ISBN 978-1-949085-07-5 (softcover)
ISBN 978-1-949085-04-4 (hardcover)
ISBN 978-1-949085-08-2 (ebook)

CKBook Publishing
PO Box 214
New Glarus, WI
53574
ckbookspublishing.com

copyright © 2018 Christine Keleny
All rights reserved

To my
Young Readers

𝓕𝒾𝓃: What are chakras, you ask? Well, we are the chakra fairies, and we are here to help explain just that!

𝓡𝓊𝒷𝓎: Chakras [chaak-ras] are places in your body that are associated with a special energy, an energy that is hard to see and hard to feel but is there none-the-less. That's why we call it magic. It is an energy that helps you every day, so it's important to make sure that the energy in each chakra is strong and energized so it can help your body and your mind work like they were designed to. (Check out the energy exercise in the back of the book if you want to get an idea of what this energy can feel like.)

Chakras need your attention much like the physical parts of your body (your muscles, heart, and lungs, for example), which need good food and lots of exercise to keep them working well. There are many ways to help your chakras do what they are supposed to do. Just like for your physical body, eating food that is good for you, exercising, or dancing can help your chakras. But also taking a walk outside or being artistic: singing, creating music, painting, are examples of other ways to help your chakras. Those are all good things to do, but I am going to explain a different way to keep your chakras working their best, a way that helps connect your mind, body, and spirit to these energy centers directly.

Sam: I'll give you a hint; you do this by using you mind and your breath.

Lilly: Two things everyone has (though not everyone uses).

Darrius: But don't you think we should explain a bit more about chakras first?

Lilly: Be my guest.

Darrius: Thank you.

You might be interested to know that the energy focused in our chakras has been talked about for hundreds of years and within many cultures. In India this energy is called prana or "life force." In China it's called chi [chee or k-eye] and qi [key]. It is ki [key] in Japan. Even Native Americans talk about the energy centers of the body.

Ruby: The energy in the chakras is sometimes described as vibrating or having a certain frequency. And each chakra has its own unique (or one of a kind) vibration or frequency [free-kwin-see]. That is why each chakra is known to have a certain color (or frequency of light wave) that goes with it. Together these colors look much like a rainbow.

Samantha: I like rainbows.

Tucker: Me too.

Rachel: But what's really important to explain is that when the energy in your chakras is not moving (or vibrating) like it should, it can affect your mind and your body.

Fin: Tell them how many chakras we have.

Rachel: I'm getting to it, just hold your horses.

Samantha: Is that the same thing as **keep your pants on**?

Tucker: I'm wearing pants.

Rachel: Keep your pants on and hold your horses are figures of speech. A figure of speech (also known as – a.k.a. – an idiom [id-e-um]) are words that don't really mean what they normally mean.

Ruby: Who thought that up?

Lilly: Adults, of course.

Ruby: Of course.

Darrius: Let's get back to chakras, already!

Samantha: Good idea.

Rachel: There are twenty-eight chakras in your body, but there are seven main chakras, just like the seven of us.

Lilly: Ruby, why don't you go first since you're the first chakra fairy.

Ruby: I'd be happy to.

The first chakra is called the base chakra or root chakra. This energy center is located at the base of your tailbone but within your body. As roots in a tree, your base chakra is the foundation of your energy system. It draws its energy from the earth through our feet and legs. It helps us with our connection to nature.

The color of the root chakra is a bright ruby-red: the lowest frequency of visible light. (Now you know how I got my name.) Because it is our base or foundation, it is like a house; when it is working well, we feel safe and we know that we will be cared for – we will have enough money, food, water, and anything else we need to feel safe and taken care of. If you were a tree and your roots weren't strong, the tree would fall over.

I think the root chakra is pretty important, don't you?!

Samantha: Well, the second chakra is pretty important too. It's called the sacral [say-krual] chakra. This energy center within your body is located a couple inches below your belly button (about four fingers down). This chakra is related to the energy of our creativity and our relationships [re-lay-shun-ships] (or interactions [in-ter-ack-shons]) with other people, with what we eat, and with what we drink. I'd say that's pretty important. It's nice to have friends or family to talk to. And it's not good for you to eat or drink to much or too little for that matter.

The color of the sacral chakra is a lovely shade of orange – just like the fruit. When your sacral chakra is vibrating its bright orange light, you feel happy and you want to share that good feeling with others. We can also use that joyful energy to be creative – sing a song, paint a picture, run and play! It will also be easier to eat and drink in ways that make your body feel better (eating and drinking things that make your physical body work better) because that will make you happy too.

Fin: You can't forget the third chakra. It's called the solar plexus [so-lar plex-sus] chakra. This energy center is located a couple inches above your belly button – the same four fingers worth. You can't really function very well if this chakra is messed up because this chakra is related directly to **you**: your feelings about yourself and your personal power. It is also where the energy from the earth and the energy from the sky (or universe) meet. That's a pretty special place, if you ask me.

The color of this chakra is a fiery yellow. When your solar plexus chakra is working well, you feel good about yourself, you feel calm, and you feel strong (I'm not talking about muscle strength, I'm talking about a personal power kind of strength – the kind of personal strength a superhero like Wonderwoman has or a man like Abraham Lincoln has).

Sometimes you might hear someone say they feel centered. That means they feel in control of themselves; they are sure of themselves and what they are doing, but at the same time they aren't afraid to ask for help when they need it – now that takes personal strength! People also talk of a getting a 'gut feeling' about something. That is their solar plexus, or true self, talking quietly to them, so they probable should listen.

Rachel: True, but the fourth chakra, the heart chakra, really gives meaning to everything we do. You can't get much more important than that. Let me explain.

The heart chakra is located in the middle of your chest. This energy center connects your physical self to the spiritual part of you, which is sometimes called your higher self or your higher consciousness [con-shuss-ness]. (That's a mouthful of letters!) This higher self is a little harder to understand, perhaps, because it is something we don't usually pay attention to, but it's a very important part of who we are.

The color of the heart chakra is emerald green – the color of new grass. When the heart chakra is working like it should, we easily feel compassion (feeling like you want to help someone or something). We easily feel love for others, nature, and sometimes more importantly, we easily feel love for ourselves. This chakra helps us feel more connected to other people, to nature, and to a higher power (which some people call God or the Divine or Source – or pure love). See what I mean about being important!

love
connecting

Tucker: But what good is all that and self-power and happiness and to the earth if we can't talk well? The fifth chakra is the throat chakra. And like it sounds, it's located within your body at the base of your neck (or throat), right above your chest bone.

The energy in the throat chakra is related to how we express ourselves: what we say and how we say it. The color of this chakra is a beautiful sky blue. When we are speaking easily, truthfully (listening to our "gut" – okay maybe the solar plexus chakra is important), and with compassion (listening to our heart and thinking of others – like the heart chakra helps us do), then our throat chakra is working well. But don't think this mean you talk all the time. It means when you talk, you can talk about what is important to you but in a way that doesn't hurt anyone else (with compassion).

Lilly: You'll want to learn about the sixth chakra, too. It is called the brow chakra, also called the third eye chakra. It is located between your eyebrows (which is probably why it's called the brow chakra). It's also called the third eye chakra because the energy here connects us to an inner knowing – our intuition [in-two-ish-shun] – (or our inner "seeing," as in: *"Ah, I see," said the woman when she figured out the problem*).

It is the center of our wisdom. Wisdom means you understand things as if you had the mind of lots and lots of different people all put together. The color frequency for this chakra is a deep, rich blue. When our brow chakra is working well, it's easier to make decisions, to trust our inner voice – to trust what our gut is whispering to us – because we have a better feeling about things; we somehow know that it is the right thing to do. We can more easily think with our heart and inner voice (or our 'gut') instead of with our minds (sometimes called our ego). So if your mind is racing like a guinea pig on an exercise wheel: thinking and thinking and thinking something about and not being able to decide, your third eye chakra may need a little attention.

𝒟𝒶𝓇𝓇𝒾𝓊𝓈: The last major charka is called the crown chakra for obvious reasons; it sits within your body at the top, or crown, of your head. And just like a king's or queen's crown, it's pretty special, indeed. This chakra is where you connect to the Divine that Rachel mentioned earlier (or God or Source or pure love) and connects you to the infinite [in-fin-it] "out there," or maybe you'd call it the Universe. (I'm not talking about religion, but many religions talk about this higher power.)

The color vibration of this chakra is a royal purple. (Are you getting the king and queen vibration here?)

When the crown chakra is working well, we can sense and trust our connection to a power/energy/force that is infinite – much, much bigger than ourselves. Like the root chakra, the crown chakra helps us feel safe. It also lets us know that we are never alone, that the Divine is part of us and that we are connected to so much more than just our physical body. Now I ask you, what is more important than that?

Ruby: If we are being honest, each chakra is just as important as the other.

Lilly: And they all work together.

Rachel: It's hard to imagine a rainbow without the red or the blue or the yellow or . . . . Well, you get the idea.

Ruby: Now, we promised to tell you how to connect to and help your seven chakras work better to keep you healthy and happy, so let's get started!

Fin: Wait a minute. First we have to talk about breathing.

Tucker: Everyone knows how to breathe. Why do we have to talk about that? Let's just get to the good part.

Samantha: You can't get to 'the good part' if you don't breathe.

Tucker: I repeat, everyone can breathe!

Samantha: Well, it works a lot **better** if you breathe a certain way.

Tucker: Better is good. Okay, go ahead.

Samantha: Thank you.

Fin: So, a Big and important part of this mind exercise to help your chakras work their best is breathing. I'm not talking about just any kind of breathing; I'm talking about deep breathing, a.k.a. – also know as - diaphragmatic [die-a-fra-ma-tic] breathing – say that seven times fast! That means slowly pulling air in through your nose until your lower belly balloons way out and feels like it is full of air. (It isn't full of air, it just feels like it is.) Then you either let the air back out through your mouth or back out through your nose, whatever feels easiest to you.

Try it a few times. If it helps, put a hand over your belly, just below your belly button. Take a slow breath in through your nose, pushing your belly (and your hand) out, then slowly let all the air out again. Try it a few more times, breathing in . . . and breathing out. Once you've got this down, you're ready for the mind exercise.

Ruby: You can do this next part by reading each section, one at a time, then trying it, or better yet, you can ask someone else to read this for you.
Darrius: You can even record yourself reading this, then close your eyes and listen to yourself.
Tucker: I don't like the recorded sound of my voice. It sounds different than when I'm listening to myself talk.
Lilly: That's because you when you listen to yourself talk, you hear with your ears and with the bones in your head. When you listen to a recording of your voice, you're only listening with your ears.

Samantha: I would ask my mom or dad to read it to me. I like to listen to them read.
Fin: Me too.
Tucker: You can do whatever you want.
Samantha: Okay, thanks.
Lilly: Oh, one more thing. The three dots.

Darrius: Also called ellipsis [e-lips-sis].

Lilly: Thank you. Yes, also called ellipsis. It means you should pause a few seconds before reading on.

Fin: Got it.

Lilly: Great!

Tucker: I'll start since I'm the talker, after all.

To start, sit or lay down in a comfortable position, a position that will allow you to relax and not think about what your body is doing or feeling. Whatever works best for you. You want to be in a place where you won't be bothered by other people or other sounds, so you can concentrate on your chakras.

Now take three, slow, deep belly breaths, breathing in . . . and breathing out. Breathing in . . . and breathing out. One more, breathing in . . . and breathing out. If your mind is really racing, then take a few more breaths. Go ahead. We're in no hurry.

You are now in a deeper state of being where you can easily let your body relax. Allow a warm wave to move through you, starting at the top of your head, moving through you, relaxing every muscle and every joint on its way down your body and into your legs, all the way down to your toes. In this place you can let go of all the things that are bothering you or that you're thinking about. If random thoughts come into your mind, you can easily push then away with the air you breathe out, as if the thoughts are captured inside a balloon that drifts effortlessly away from you with each breath out.

Ruby: Now, turn your attention to the very base of your body, to your root chakra. This is inside your body but at the level of your tailbone. It is a swirling ruby-red color that grows brighter with every slow breath you take. It is the place that connects you to the energy of the earth and to nature and helps you get what you need.

Say to yourself or out loud:

I am connected to the earth . . .
I am safe . . .
I am taken care of . . .
I trust that I will get what I need . . .

And so it is.

*

Now take another deep breath.

Samantha: The energy of the root chakra easily pushes you up to the level of your sacral chakra, about four fingers below your belly button. The sacral chakra glows with a lovely orange color that grows larger and stronger with every breath you take. This is the energy that you use to connect with others, with the things around you like what you eat and what you drink, and with your creativity.

Say to yourself or out loud:

> I have good relationships with friends and family . . .
> I have a good relationship with what I eat and drink . . .
> These relationships make me happy . . .
> And help me be creative in many different ways . . .

And so it is.

Now take another deep breath.

𝓕𝒾𝓃: Focus your attention four fingers above your belly button to your solar plexus chakra. Your solar plexus chakra is a fiery yellow color. It is where you can feel your personal power, a power that makes it easier to do things that are helpful to you and allows you be your true self. Imagine yourself sitting on a beach, the warm yellow sun warming you and making you smile. Any stray thoughts or fears you might have are carried up to the sun and disappear in its firery brightness.

Say to yourself or out loud:

I feel good about myself . . .
I feel strong and centered . . .
I have personal power . . .
That I use to help myself and others . . .

And so it is.
*
Now take a deep breath.

Rachel: Next, turn your thoughts to the place in the middle of your chest. This is your heart chakra. It is the color of new green grass. With every breath you take, the green color glows brighter and stronger. The heart chakra helps you love and connect with your parents, your friends, even people you don't know. You care about everyone and everything around you. It is a place that also helps you to love yourself because you are love.

Say to yourself or out loud:

I love others and I love myself . . .
I use love in everything I do . . .
Love makes me happy . . .
I am love . . .

And so it is.

*

Now take a deep breath.

Tucker: The energy in your heart chakra draws you easily up to the base of your throat or your throat chakra. Your throat chakra glows with the color of a clear blue sky. It grows brighter and larger with each breath you take. This is where you connect with the energy of your true voice. It is where you talk about what is true for you: what is important to you, what you feel is true, but you do this without hurting others.

Say to yourself or out loud:

I am able to say what I mean . . .
I can do this without hurting others . . .
I listen before I speak . . .
I am grateful every day . . .

And so it is.
*
Now take a deep breath.

𝓛𝓲𝓵𝓵𝔂: Focus your attention to the place between your eyebrows, to your brow chakra or third eye chakra. Your third eye chakra is a deep blue color that gets stronger and grows each time you take a breath. It is the energy you use to listen to the little voice inside you, the thoughts that comes from your gut and from your heart. It helps you "see" the answer to questions you have.

Say to yourself or out loud:

> I am able to listen to my inner voice . . .
> I trust what my gut and my heart tell me . . .
> I can look beyond what I see . . .
> I see possibilities everywhere . . .

And so it is.
*
Now take a deep breath.

𝒟𝒶𝓇𝓇𝒾𝓊𝓈: Move your thought to inside the top of your head where your crown chakra sits. Your crown chakra swirls with rich purple color that gets larger and richer with each breath you take. This is where you connect with the Higher Power or God and where you connect with everything outside of you: the earth, the universe

Say to yourself or out loud.

I am connected to a power that is bigger than me . . .
I use that connection to help me every day . . .
That connection is always with me . . .
It is part of who I am . . .

And so it is.
✳

𝒯𝓊𝒸𝓀𝑒𝓇: Now take a deep breath in and notice that your seven chakras are all glowing a bright rainbow of color from the top of your head to the base of your spine. They are strong and able to help you perform your best every day.

Take one more deep breath and as you breathe out, slowly move your hands and your feet, bringing your attention back into the room you are in. And when you are ready, slowly open your eyes, feeling completely calm and ready for whatever life has to offer you.

Energy exercise

Lilly: I'm going to show you how to feel the energy we've been talking about.

One way to do this is to sit up straight and take three, slow deep breaths – breathing in . . . and breathing out. Breathing in . . . and breathing out, focusing on the air as it comes into your body, then as it flows easily out. One more – breathing in . . . and breathing out.

Now close your eyes and lift your hands so they are sitting comfortably in front of you. Turn you hands so the palms face each other, just a couple inches apart but not touching each other. Concentrate on the space between your hands. Does it feel like there is something there, between your hands? Don't worry if you don't feel anything. Continue concentrating on the space between your hands.

Take a deep breath in and let it out. Very slowly move your hands apart a few more inches. Does it feel like there is something there trying to pull them back together again?

Slowly move your hands back toward each other but don't let them touch. Does it feel like there is something pressing together between your hands?

Take another deep breath in and let it out and open your eyes.

Don't worry if you can't feel anything the first time you try this, just try it another day.

Sometimes it's fun to try with another person as you sit in front of each other – both of their hands facing both of your hands but not touching.
Repeat the same execise above.

About the Author

Christine is an award-winning author, a reader, editor, book designer and publisher. She loves writing and helping others publish the book of their dreams through her publishing company: CKBooks Publishing. Christine also teaches workshops at local libraries for both youth and adults and a youth writing and publishing summer school class. You can find all of her books at christinekelenybooks.com. You can learn about her middle grade mystery adventure series at AgnesKellyMysteryAdventures.com. The websites are also where you can sign up for her Readers' Group.

If you enjoyed this book, please consider writing a review on your favorite website. Reviews are a great help to independent authors such as Christine, and she would like to know what you think ~ really!

About the Illustrator

Born in Venezuela, Marianella Aguirre, an only child, spent much of her time drawing while traveling to the United States and other countries with her mother.

She is a multicultural traveling career illustrator for the youth and has lived in far away countries. Each country's cultures and lifestyles are reflected in her illustrations.

Marianella has earned three University degrees. She started studying to be an engineer but after two years she realized her dream was to continue her studies to become a graphic designer and illustrator.

Like a good disciplined artist, Marianella dominates in diverse technical skills and styles: patchwork, sculptures, knitting, clay figures, bears and much more.

Marianella has won various prizes and is published in more than ninety books in English, Arabic and Spanish. Without a doubt, Marianella illustrates with the same enthusiasm with which she encounters life.

Marianella currently lives in New Zealand after ten years in Spain.

www.ingramcontent.com/pod-product-compliance
Lightning Source LLC
Chambersburg PA
CBHW042356280426
43661CB00096B/1137